THE DETROIT RED WINGS

KURT WALDENDORF

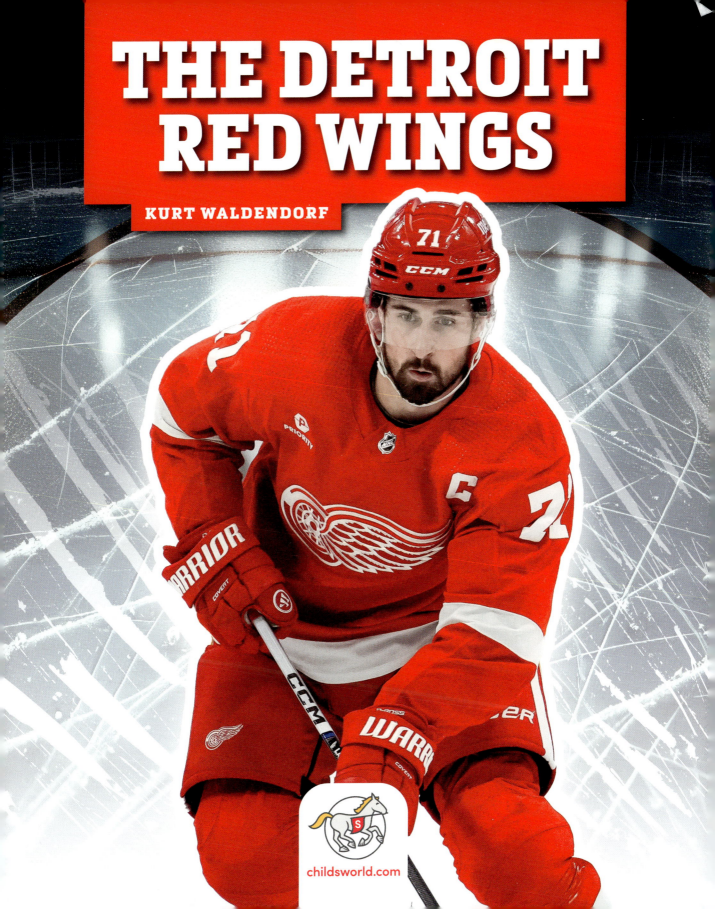

childsworld.com

The Child's World®
childsworld.com

Published by The Child's World®
800-599-READ • www.childsworld.com

Photography Credits
Cover: ©Nic Antaya/Getty Images; multiple pages: ©Hanna Siamashka/iStock/Getty Images; GLYPHstock/iStock/Getty Images; md tauhidul/Shutterstock; page 5: ©Dave Reginek/NHLI/Getty Images; page 6: ©Bettmann/Getty Images; page 9: ©Brice Bennett/Getty Images; page 10: ©Jennifer Hefner/Dave Reginek/NHLI/Getty Images; page 12: ©Mike Mulholland/Getty Images; page 12: ©Minas Panagiotakis/Getty Images; page 13: ©Melchior DiGiacomo/Getty Images; page 13: ©Bruce Bennett/Bruce Bennett Studios/Getty Images; page 14: ©Dave Reginek/NHLI/Getty Images; page 16: ©Bruce Bennett Studios via Getty Images Studios/Getty Images; page 16: ©Collection/Bruce Bennett Studios/Getty Images; page 17: ©Focus on Sport/Getty Images; page 17: ©John Russell/NHLI/Getty Images; page 18: ©Bruce Bennett Studios via Getty Images Studios/Getty Images; page 18: ©Albert Dickson/Sporting News Archive/Getty Images; page 19: ©Bruce Bennett/Getty Images for NHL/Getty Images; page 19: ©John Russell/NHLI/Getty Images: page 20: ©Nic Antaya/Getty Images; page 20: ©Dave Reginek/NHLI/Getty Images; page 21: ©Minas Panagiotakis/Getty Images; page 21: ©Dave Reginek/NHLI/Getty Images; page 22: ©Bettmann/Getty Images; page 23: ©Jeff Vinnick/NHLI/Getty Images; page 25: ©Harry How/Getty Images; page 26: ©Jim McIsaac/Getty Images; page 29: ©Jonathan Daniel/Getty Images

ISBN Information
9781503870727 (Reinforced Library Binding)
9781503871908 (Portable Document Format)
9781503873148 (Online Multi-user eBook)
9781503874381 (Electronic Publication)

LCCN
Library of Congress Control Number: 2024950381

Printed in the United States of America

BRINGING THE WORLD
19 68
TO YOUNG READERS

ABOUT THE AUTHOR
Kurt Waldendorf is the author of more than a dozen books for children. When he's not writing or editing, he enjoys indoor rock climbing and running along the shore of Lake Michigan with his dog. He lives in Chicago.

CONTENTS

Go Red Wings!

The Detroit Red Wings compete in the National Hockey League's (NHL) Eastern Conference. They play in the Atlantic **Division** with the Boston Bruins, Buffalo Sabres, Florida Panthers, Montreal Canadiens, Ottawa Senators, Tampa Bay Lightning, and Toronto Maple Leafs. The Red Wings are one of the oldest teams in the NHL. Their fans have been lucky! The Red Wings have appeared in the NHL playoffs 64 times. The team has won 11 Stanley Cups. Let's learn more about the Red Wings.

Eastern Conference • Atlantic Division

Boston Bruins	Detroit Red Wings	Montreal Canadiens	Tampa Bay Lightning
Buffalo Sabres	Florida Panthers	Ottawa Senators	Toronto Maple Leafs

The Red Wings are one of the NHL's most popular teams. Fans refer to Detroit as "Hockeytown."

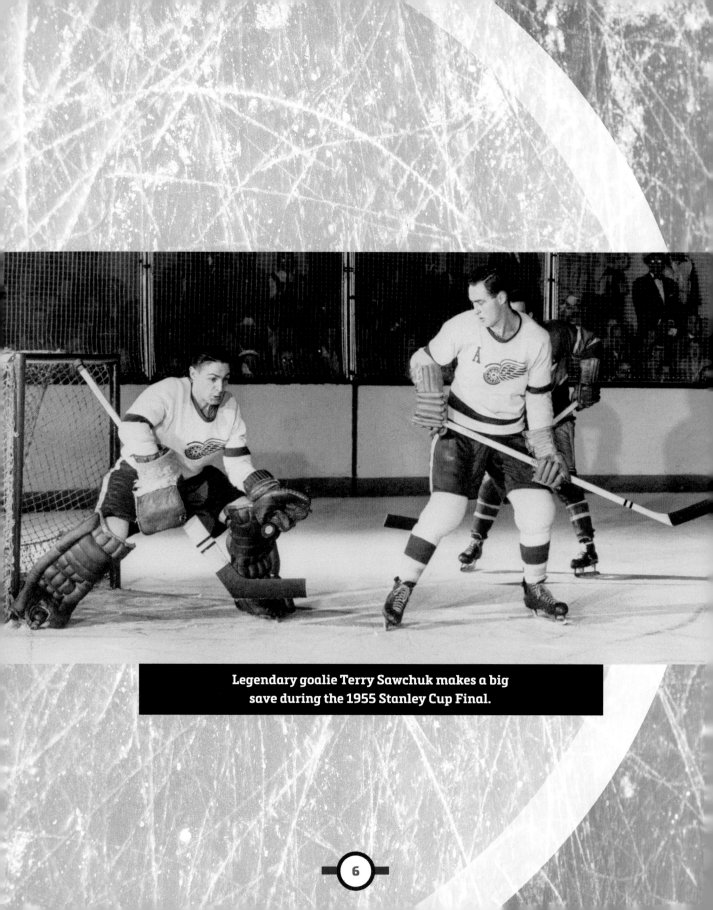

Legendary goalie Terry Sawchuk makes a big save during the 1955 Stanley Cup Final.

Becoming the Red Wings

The Red Wings played their first season in 1926. Led by **Hall of Fame** player Syd Howe, the team found early success. They won titles in 1936, 1937, and 1943. In the 1950s, the Wings continued to thrive. Two of the best players of all time led the team. Winger Gordie Howe and goaltender Terry Sawchuk brought the Wings to four more Stanley Cup titles. From 1967 to 1983, the team struggled. They went to the playoffs only two times. Fans nicknamed the team the "Dead Wings." In the 1990s, Center Steve Yzerman and coach Scotty Bowman helped bring life back to the team. Detroit won titles in 1997 and 1998. In the 2000s, the team added two more with the help of defenseman Nicklas Lidström and center Pavel Datsyuk. In recent years, the Wings have struggled. But with young stars Moritz Seider and Lucas Raymond, the future looks bright.

By the Numbers

The Red Wings have had lots of success on the ice. Below is some information about the team's success throughout history.

 The Red Wings have won 11 Stanley Cups, the most of any team based in the United States.

 The team has earned a total of 29 division titles. **29**

 The team's best regular season was in 1996. They won 62 games, which is tied for second-most ever by an NHL team. **62**

 The Red Wings have reached the playoffs 64 times. **64**

The Red Wings celebrate their 11th Stanley Cup win in 2008.

Little Caesars Arena holds 19,515 hockey fans for Red Wings games. The team shares the arena with basketball's Detroit Pistons.

Game Night

Detroit's stadium was not ready for the 1926 season. So the team played at an arena in Windsor, Canada. The city is just across the border from Michigan. The Red Wings moved back to Detroit in 1927. They played in Olympia Stadium and later, in Joe Louis Arena. In 2017, the team moved into Little Caesars Arena. Outside of the arena, there is a covered area called the Via. It features restaurants and shops. It also has statues and murals of Red Wings greats.

We're Famous!

The Red Wings logo is one of the most well-known in sports. It shows a wheel with wings. The image represents Detroit's car-making business. The logo shows off the pride people have in their state. Famous Michigan musicians such as Kid Rock and Eminem have often worn Red Wings gear. The logo has also often appeared on the big screen. One of the most famous examples is in the 1980s hit movie *Ferris Bueller's Day Off*. One of the characters wears a Gordie Howe jersey throughout the movie.

Uniforms

HOME

AWAY

Goalie Gear

For years, NHL goalies did not wear masks. As a result, they often got hit with pucks. Red Wings goalie Terry Sawchuk did not wear a mask for 16 years. In 1962, he decided he'd had enough of getting hit in the face. He became the first Wings goalie to protect his face during games. Goalie masks like Sawchuk's were plain. In 1973, Jim Rutherford changed things up. He wore a white mask with red wings over each eye. Rutherford didn't like the design at first. But he found success wearing it. It became one of the most well-known masks in goalie history.

Truly Weird

From 1989 to 1990, the Red Wings picked three Russian players in the NHL **Draft**. But there was a problem. The players could not freely travel to the United States. In the early 1990s, the United States and Russia did not get along. Bringing the players to Detroit was a hard task. The team had to communicate with the players in secret. They had to pay **bribes** to get the players out of Russia. By 1992, the three players had arrived in Detroit. They were joined in 1995 by two other Russian players. The group became known as the Russian Five. They helped the Wings win titles in 1997 and 1998.

Team Spirit

Detroit fans have always been passionate about their team. In 1952, the team had won seven-straight games in the playoffs. They were one win away from winning the Stanley Cup. Early in the game, two fans threw a dead octopus onto the ice. Its eight legs represented the eight wins the team needed to win the title. The Wings went on to win the game. The Legend of the Octopus was born. Over the years, fans continued to throw dead octopuses onto the ice. In the 1990s, a stadium worker named Al Sobotka started twirling an octopus over his head between periods. As a result, the team's official mascot became Al the Octopus in 1995. In recent years, new traditions have started. Fans often sing the song "Don't Stop Believin'" by Journey in the third period. The song helps energize the team, inspiring them to finish strong.

The Red Wings' official mascot is Al the Octopus, but there is no costumed octopus mascot—only a giant inflatable Al that lives in the rafters of Little Caesars Arena.

Heroes of History

Terry Sawchuk
Goaltender | 1949–1955, 1957–1964, 1968–1969

Terry Sawchuk achieved a lot as a Red Wing. He won four Stanley Cup titles. He was named the top goaltender in the league four times. And he set NHL records for career **shutouts**, games played, and wins. Unfortunately, Sawchuk died in 1970 at the age of 40. Though his career was cut short, he left a lasting mark on the league. His exciting, aggressive play style changed how goalies played the position. In 1971, Sawchuk was added to the Hockey Hall of Fame.

Alex Delvecchio
Center | 1950–1974

Alex Delvecchio was a superstar many NHL fans didn't know about. While other top players sought attention, Delvecchio kept to himself. On the ice, he didn't pick fights or take penalties. In fact, he won the league's award for **sportsmanship** three times. Still, Delvecchio was a strong scorer. His 1,281 points rank third in team history. In 1974, Delvecchio retired after 24 seasons with the Red Wings. In 1977, he finally got the national attention he deserved. He was selected to the Hockey Hall of Fame.

Steve Yzerman
1983–2006 | Center

When the Red Wings drafted Steve Yzerman with their top pick in 1983, they hoped he could turn the team around. Yzerman delivered. In his first season, the **rookie** scored a team-best 87 points. He helped bring the team back to the playoffs. In 1986, he was named team captain at age 21. Under his leadership, the team went to the playoffs 18 of 19 seasons. They won three Stanley Cups. When Yzerman retired in 2006, he was the team's second-leading scorer of all time and still holds this record. He hadn't just turned the team. He'd become an all-time great.

Nicklas Lidström
1991–2012 | Defenseman

While Yzerman led the Wings' offense, Nicklas Lidström was the defensive leader. In his first season, he was named to the All-Rookie team. But he was just getting started. He went on to be named the league's top defender seven times, which is the second-most in the league. In 2006, Lidström took over as team captain when Yzerman retired. Lidström brought the team to another title in 2008, his fourth. Lidström retired in 2012. In 2015, he was selected to the Hockey Hall of Fame.

Big Days

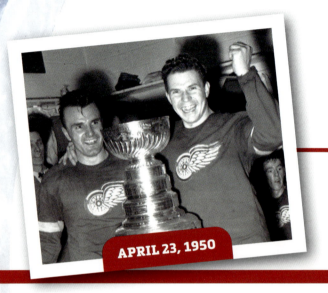

APRIL 23, 1950

The Red Wings beat the New York Rangers for their fourth Stanley Cup.

The Red Wings win their first title in 42 years and their eighth overall. The team is led by Steve Yzerman and winger Sergei Fedorov.

JUNE 7, 1997

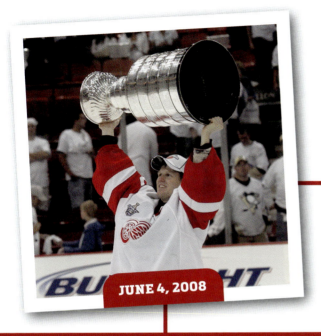

JUNE 4, 2008

Led by Nicklas Lidström and goaltender Chris Osgood, the Red Wings win their 11th Stanley Cup title over the Pittsburgh Penguins.

The Red Wings begin a record-setting winning streak. Led by Pavel Datsyuk, Henrik Zetterberg, and Nicklas Lidström, the team wins 23-straight home games.

NOVEMBER 5, 2011

Modern-Day Marvels

Dylan Larkin
Center | 2015–Present

Dylan Larkin was picked in the first round of the 2014 NHL Draft. The team had high hopes for the 19-year-old. He made a difference right away. In his rookie season, he led the team in goals. In 2016, he was selected for the All-Star game. During the All-Star skills competition, he set a record for fastest skater. But Larkin isn't just quick on his feet. He's also a strong leader. In 2020, Larkin was named team captain. In 2022 and 2023, he was selected for his second and third All-Star appearances.

Alex DeBrincat
Right Wing | 2023–Present

Alex DeBrincat grew up a Red Wings fan in Michigan. In 2016, he was drafted by the Chicago Blackhawks. Then, in 2023, he was traded to his home state's team. The Red Wings hoped the small, quick winger could bring some scoring to the team. In his first season, he delivered. He scored 67 points and was selected to the All-Star game.

Lucas Raymond
Left Wing | 2021–Present

Joining Larkin on the top **line** is Lucas Raymond. The Swedish winger was picked fourth overall in the 2020 NHL Draft. As a result, the team had big expectations for him. In his first season with the team, he lived up to the hype. Raymond scored 57 points. He was selected to the All-Rookie team. Since then, he has continued to grow. In 2024, he led the team with 72 points.

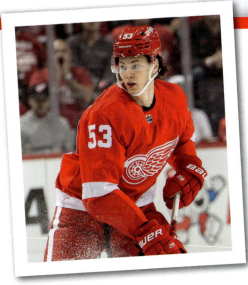

Moritz Seider
Defenseman | 2021–Present

On the defensive end, Moritz Seider is an up-and-coming star. Seider was Detroit's top pick in the 2019 Draft. In 2022, the German defenseman scored 50 points. He was named to the All-Rookie team. He also won the award for top rookie of the year. In recent years, Seider has become stronger. At 6 feet, 3 inches (1.9 m), he is a tough defender. The team hopes he will help protect the goal for many years to come.

Gordie Howe's 801 goals are third-most in NHL history.
Howe is Detroit's leader in both goals (786) and points (1,809).

The G.O.A.T.

Known as "Mr. Hockey," Gordie Howe wasn't just a good scorer. He was tough. In 1950, he hit his head on the boards. People worried his career might be over. But he came back from the injury the following season. Howe helped the Red Wings win four Stanley Cup titles. He led the league in scoring six times and won six Most Valuable Player (MVP) awards. Howe was selected to the NHL Hall of Fame in 1972.

Fan Favorite

For years, Red Wings fans disliked Chris Chelios. He played for the **rival** Chicago Blackhawks. He was a tough player. He pushed Red Wings players around. Then, in 1999, Chelios was traded from Chicago to Detroit. Over time, Red Wings fans saw a different side of Chelios. They learned he was a hard worker. He set a good example. He played tough to help protect his teammates on the ice. In his 10 seasons with the Red Wings, he went from rival to fan favorite.

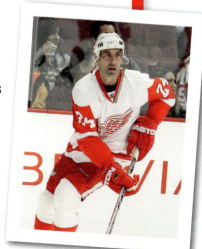

The Big Game

The 2002 Red Wings had amazing talent. The team included 10 Hall of Fame players. The coach, Scotty Bowman, was thought to be the best of all time. The team had an excellent regular season. Could they meet their full potential in the playoffs? The answer came in the third game of the Stanley Cup Final. The series with the Carolina Hurricanes was split one game to one. Whoever won Game 3 would have the upper hand in the series. The game was hard fought. With just over a minute left in regulation, Detroit tied the score. Then, in the third **overtime** period, Igor Larionov scored the winner for the Wings. The team would go on to win the next two games. The title was Detroit's third in six years. It assured the team's place as one of the best of all time.

Igor Larionov scored five goals during the 2002 playoffs, but his winning shot in Game 3 is the most memorable.

In his 20 seasons with the Red Wings, Nicklas Lidström scored 264 goals and logged 1,142 points.

Amazing Feats

Most Shutouts

Terry Sawchuk tallied 12 shutouts in three different seasons from 1952 to 1955. During the same period, he was named top goalie in the league twice.

12

Most Penalty Minutes

In the 1987–1988 season, winger Bob Probert played the role of enforcer, playing tough, physical hockey to help set up the team's scorers. In the process, he racked up a total of 398 penalty minutes.

398

Points By a Defenseman

In 2005–2006, defenseman Nicklas Lidström scored 16 goals and had 64 assists for a total of 80 points. Lidström was named the top defender in the league for the fourth time.

80

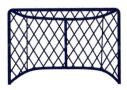

Most Power Play Goals

Two Red Wings have scored 21 **power play** goals in a season. Winger Mickey Redmond did it in 1974. Winger Dino Ciccarelli did it in 1993.

21

All-Time Best

MOST POINTS

1	Gordie Howe	1,809
2	Steve Yzerman	1,755
3	Alex Delvecchio	1,281
4	Nicklas Lidström	1,142
5	Henrik Zetterberg	960

HAT TRICKS

1	Gordie Howe	19
2	Steve Yzerman	18
3	Norm Ullman	11
4	Brendan Shanahan	10
5	Syd Howe	7
	Dale McCourt	7

MOST GOALS

1	Gordie Howe	786
2	Steve Yzerman	692
3	Alex Delvecchio	456
4	Sergei Fedorov	400
5	Henrik Zetterberg	337

SAVES

1	Jimmy Howard	13,970
2	Chris Osgood	12,801
3	Terry Sawchuk	10,376
4	Roger Crozier	8,002
5	Jim Rutherford	7,874

MOST ASSISTS

1	Steve Yzerman	1,063
2	Gordie Howe	1,023
3	Nicklas Lidström	878
4	Alex Delvecchio	825
5	Henrik Zetterberg	623

SHUTOUTS

1	Terry Sawchuk	85
2	Chris Osgood	39
3	Harry Lumley	26
4	Jimmy Howard	24
5	Dominik Hašek	20

Jimmy Howard attempts a big save during a 2013 game against the Chicago Blackhawks.

GLOSSARY

bribes (BRYBZ) Bribes are amounts of money people pay to persuade others to do something.

division (dih-VIZSH-un) A division is a group of teams within the NHL that compete with each other to have the best record each season and advance to the playoffs.

draft (DRAFT) A draft is a yearly event when teams take turns choosing new players. In the NHL, teams can select North American ice hockey players between the ages of 18 and 20 and international players between 18 and 21 to join the league.

Hall of Fame (HAHL of FAYM) The Hockey Hall of Fame is a museum in Ontario, Canada. The best players and coaches in the game are honored there.

line (LYN) A line in hockey is made up of a center, left winger, and right winger who are on the ice at the same time.

overtime (OH-vur-tym) Overtime is extra time added to the end of a game when the regular time is up and the score is tied.

power play (POW-uhr PLAY) A power play occurs when a player gets a penalty and the other team has more players on the ice.

rival (RYE-vuhl) A rival is a team's top competitor, which they try to outdo and play better than each season.

rookie (ROOK-ee) A rookie is a new or first-year player in a professional sport.

shutout (SHUT-owt) A shutout occurs when a goalie keeps the other team from scoring any goals.

sportsmanship (SPORTS-muhn-ship) Sportsmanship is when people playing a sport treat each other with respect.

FAST FACTS

- The Detroit area is known as "Hockeytown" because of its passionate fan base.

- The team was known as the Cougars and the Falcons in its early years. In 1932, the team adopted the Red Wings name and logo.

- The Red Wings went on an amazing run from 1991 to 2016. The team made the playoffs 25 seasons in a row.

- The Red Wings have honored eight players by retiring their jersey numbers. The players are Gordie Howe, Terry Sawchuk, Steve Yzerman, Alex Delvecchio, Nicklas Lidström, Ted Lindsay, Sid Abel, and Red Kelly.

ONE STRIDE FURTHER

- Gordie Howe scored 801 goals in the NHL and 174 in the World Hockey Association, another pro league. Wayne Gretzky scored 894 NHL goals. Which player do you think should be called the goal leader and why?

- Based on what you've learned from this book, what do you think it takes for a team to win the Stanley Cup? Is it great scoring? Excellent defenders? A top goalie? What about leadership? Discuss your opinion with a friend.

- Players around the world train hard to make it to the NHL. Write a paragraph describing the skills and attitudes you think it takes to reach the highest level.

- Ask friends and family members to name their favorite sport to watch and their favorite sport to play. Keep track and make a graph to see which sports are the most popular.

FIND OUT MORE

IN THE LIBRARY

Doeden, Matt. *G.O.A.T. Hockey Teams*. Minneapolis, MN: Lerner, 2021.

Doeden, Matt. *The Stanley Cup Playoffs*. Minneapolis, MN: Lerner, 2020.

Graves, Will. *Pro Hockey Upsets*. Minneapolis, MN: Lerner, 2020.

Laughlin, Kara L. *Hockey*. Parker, CO: The Child's World, 2024.

ON THE WEB

Visit our website for links about the Detroit Red Wings:

childsworld.com/links

Note to Parents, Caregivers, Teachers, and Librarians: We routinely verify our web links to make sure they are safe and active sites. So encourage your readers to check them out!

INDEX